Aloha America

SAVE A COUNTRY;

OURS,

THEN

WE CAN HELP OTHERS.

By

Sue Ann Scott

"Susie"

1authorsuescott@gmail.com

**"When the solution is simple,
God is answering."
--- Albert Einstein**

**Election 2016 requires our
utmost attention;
our most diligent research;
and plain commonsense.**

Aloha means

Hello or Goodbye

Please, choose Hello America

* there is one asterisk in this booklet;

find the info and write it here...

Prologue

When you are in danger of losing your Country to something like NWO, New World Order, you must be prepared to fight; however and whenever you can.

Yes, this is War.

We the People are fighting for our Country.

Our Constitution needs upheld and our Laws followed. Furthermore; this is no time for 'Spirit of the Law," This *Is* the time for 'Letter of the Law."

Table of Contents:

Chapter *book requires participation* Page

Note: I am writing this book in between pictures transferring for my first book, "Aloha Mom" that I hope to have out ASAP; although I guess not in time for my Mom's Celebration of Life on 10/22/16. Actually "Aloha Mom" was completed a month ago; however, the photos keep disappearing!

Chapter One

Is this War?

Are We the People losing what our taxes should be paying for to Corruption? YES

In this war there are no Democrats or Republicans, we are all Americans fighting towards one common goal; so well said by Djou of Hawaii, so well said by a Military man running for Congress; however, he has betrayed us, We the People. He has betrayed us as so many have, whom are supposed to be representing US. We the People must not accept Representatives who do not have American's best interest at heart. By not doing their job!

Not "quoted" because I am not sure of his exact words... Albeit, his *words* were correct, if followed-through with *that* intention.

People like the Bush Family I thought were for America... It is so heart-breaking to find out otherwise. I probably have all their photos which were sent out to supporters; albeit, I don't want to spend the postage to send photos all back to them now. They are for NWO so they are against America...

Against We the People.

I hear McCain got an earful about doing his job!

Representatives must be communicated with that they must do their job that We voted them to do. Or get them out of the Office.

We, the People must discover the people against our Constitution and Laws and get-rid-of-them. As soon as possible.

If they are not doing their job We should be able to get them out of Office.

Each person in each State needs to do their part to help clean-house in our Government.

We must remember to listen to the words; however, but heed the actions. Heed them the first time.

Words are so very important, and need thought with a heart of God to convey their true meaning; to be honest with yourself first.

But how can we know a man's heart? Simply by observing his actions, or, in-actions. They say, "Actions speak louder than words."

Observe... as well as the in-actions; however, not as easily spotted. At times; so deceitfully orchestrated to appear to be for us all the while actually being against us. Even if *that* was not the first intention, IT IS, in fact, what It becomes...for better or worse for We the People. In actuality, they may not really be against us, as much as just out for their own selves.

Same difference, as they say.

What say you?

Edward O'Brien, and ((someone else,)) said, "Money corrupts; money and power absolutely corrupts."

The power should be by We the People and the money should be at the same pay rate as our Military.

Furthermore; if we are indeed at war, to realize what will it take to win?

Representatives who love America and put America first. Commonsense.

To win our Country back to where we are proud and prosperous...for the pursuit of happiness. Such a simple thing that all Americans should be able to attain.

Worst are, and have been for years, the inner Cities.

Who can solve the problem instead of just talk? Certainly not the people who have done nothing but seemingly make things worse than you would think.

Have you heard the adage: It's not the size of the dog but the size of the fight in the dog. Well, let me add to that...the fight must be with heart. In the Case of "We the People" it is the fight in hearts of men for the Country they truly love.

We must not stand by any longer and let the rioters lead our America in the wrong direction.

So; let me ask you this... how can one love a Country and do things to break-down a Country?

Or, if they do not know that Country and believe in what that Country stands for, or against?

This simple reason of understanding should be the basis for a man going to War.

Speaking of Combat War; we need our best and strongest to be the most qualified to protect not just our Country but the man, husband, father brother right next to him in such a battle.

Normally, when speaking in generalities and of both sexes you simply say "man" referring to both genders; however, when speaking of Combat War the term "man must be expanded to mean ready, willing, and most importantly, able. Able to carry a 180 to 200 pound man of muscle, along with their firearms, an unspecified distance to safety. Or, as safe as they can be. Remembering, that man is a brother-in-arms.

It is not whether or not there is a vagina, but the strength of the biceps, triceps, back and legs... women are just not built the same; fact. Standards must never be lowered for accommodation but

hired to get the best for the safety
and security of America.

Think about *those* whom are
waiting for their safe return.
Shouldn't we send only our best, the
best qualified for the job of Combat?
Of course; with the best equipment
possible. And, never to allow
equipment to fall into enemy hands.
Which, by the way, our State
Department has allowed many times.
Concluding facts of irresponsibility, if
not Treason.

Do you realize what "Combat"
might even entail?

And those things men have seen that may not be forgotten, that every-measure will be taken to ensure the best care for those whom may have to pay the ultimate sacrifice. We the People *must* do our best to put those in the correct positions to represent the job(s) which must be done for those brave souls.

We, being Americans, must do *whatever, whenever* we can...something, anything...to help in any and every way to assist our fellow man.

What have you done lately?

A very simple example; if I may…
While I was at the Library I became
hungry and they have a little snack
bar. Well, I bought the Tuna Sandwich
and it had soggy bread. I got so mad!
No, of course not. I remembered a
trick I learned many years ago helping
to make sandwiches; very simple, just
put a little butter or margarine on the
bread and it won't get soggy. Now,
that took only a few minutes and will
make so many people more satisfied
with their food, should they choose to
do so.

In every single aspects of our
lives God gave man freewill. It is our

duty, as well-meaning Americans to do our best at every turn of life. No matter how significant/insignificant.

To put it very simple.
Do your best.

Think about it, if you do your best the first time then most likely you won't have to do it over...whatever it may be; tangible or intangible.
Think about it...

Really, think over what *you* may or may not have done which could have had a much better possibility of an outcome had you simply done your best?

Do most kids today have *this* attitude?

Sadly, the attitude of many today is gimme, gimme, gimme. And if you do not; You don't gimme you're racist. Riot, riot, riot.

What is wrong with these people? Really, we need to find out and help them.

Furthermore, you probably only created more problems for yourself, and/or others by trying to hurry, or, taking a short-cut. Or, to down right take situations hostage. Harming others to get the your gimme.

Are kids even trying to take shortcuts; or now, just rebelling. Even worse, now, causing riots.

We must remember to listen to the words; however, heed the actions. Heed them the first time.

Kids, young adults... have gotten way-out-of-hand.

This is war. War to save America and our future generations.

A war against selfishness and greed.

A war against false perceptions.

A war against the failure of our government to keep promises but also to keep out of people's personal business; if it is actually none of their business. Children are all of society's business. They are our future. And, Right now *that* is pretty scary.

With any job/career, if it is worth doing then it is worth doing well. Or at least to the best of your ability; however, if your ability is not up to/ for that particular job then have the common sense to get the correct person for that job/career.

That said; there are those whom will need extra help and monitoring to bring them up to their own God-given ability which they have lost the will to see, let alone to do.

Whether it was/is because of alcohol or drugs they will need extra help; however, they must be ready and willing to help their self also.

We can not, must not, allow the infiltration of drugs no matter how many people say that drug may help them. At the risk of losing brain cells, or immune system people are not realizing that this is *not* the correct alternative for their help.

That CPTG oils are free of THC are not only better for you but also not harmful. Wake Up America!

So Shameful to be making goodies to entice more youth and even adults, sadly, to such harmful substances containing THC. Who is wanting this?

Take a good look and do your research! Yes, *this* is war, a war against being corrupted, or even desensitized to such wrongful use.

Take marijuana, Stop any use with THC; when they can use oils without THC which will actually work better. Why would they do this to Americans... why am I repeating this? Because it just does not comprehending to some. Think about it…

Then realize that no matter how much you try to do your job well, that it will be more difficult if you are destroying brain cells, or weak because of your immune system. Commonsense.

Where has commonsense gone?

Anyone who is for harmful drugs is either uninformed, misinformed, or surely does not care about anyone but themselves and getting high.

It is amazing, and frightening, that Obama put the VP of Monsanto in-charge of our FDA.

Why even have an FDA if they can not be trusted?

People need to be trusted by a showing of their good-works. Unfortunately you cannot trust words of a person whom has been proven to have lied, or misrepresented something. Horrifying is if that person was put in-charge of something and they have done things wrong but no one does anything to them. So very wrong not to hold all those people accountable for their own job.   Like petiphilers in Priesthood. Weiner in our Senate, disgraceful. Clinton.

How-in-the-world could anyone with half-a-brain want her or him again as President...oh, literally turns my stomach.

At least, we must try, in our Government We the People must be sure, as sure as possible, to put the correct people in-charge to Represent us; USA. We are Americans.

One must discover their *passion* to be able to do their best while enjoying their job/career, or simple a task. Yes, learn to delegate as long as you are confident to delegate to the correct person/persons.

Tune-in when someone asks you your passion.

However, thinking... How can one have a passion for war? If they do, then they are not the correct person for the job. It is the passion in the heart for love of Country. The passion in the learning and executing what it takes to do the task at-hand. The passion to win for America, for We the People.

It must be the passion of being American to do what is best for fellow Americans.

Since the failure of our Administrations' for far too long, it will not be easy to overcome the years of failures. To take control of Government and our Debt. Except, that our Debt was really Grand Theft Larceny because it was not done in the best interest of America. In fact, should be named as Acts of Treason. All the people responsible should be held accountable and liable. Certainly, No immunity.

This is war...

War against those holding our Government hostage; and more so, war against those whom hate and want to destroy America.

War is on all fronts; We the People must be diligent.

Chapter Two

Which Came First; Money or Power?

To listen first...to the whisper of doing what is best for all, giving the best you know at that time.

We are not black or white, and every color in between, We Are Americans...and we must vote with the best true information available!

Talking to people; many of them say you can't find out the truth in anything anymore, it is really bad.

*((Teddy Roosevelt quote on being American)) Please look this up for yourself. It is very important. Why not put it here? Because if you take the time and effort to look it up, you will read it and take it to heart.

This is the time to, "Ask not what your Country can do for you, but what you can do for your Country." -- - John F. Kennedy

Think about that. I mean really think about it.

This *is* the time for you to ask yourself such an important question.

Used to be that we could count on our elected Representatives to do the "right thing."

When was that?

When was such a time lost?

Now We the People must fight, even with our elected Representatives, for what we want as "We the People."

Why did we lose such a time… money and power.

Maybe our Representatives should earn such pay as our Military. Aren't they fighting for US?

Well, they're supposed to be.

It is time to turn away from money and power; to turn toward The Constitution and the Bill of Rights.

To turn toward upholding our laws. No more 'Spirit of the law' until the 'letter of the law' is the law of the land and appreciated again. Yes, some things still need changed. LIKE FOLLOWING THE LAW with no exceptions especially because of so-called Political Correctness **WHICH HAS GOTTEN WAY OUT OF HAND!**

In fact, backwards it seems.

Since when has law been lost?

No more shall We the People be hood-winked by our Government.

We the People want a Stop to the corruption, and make sure our laws upheld…plain and simple.

No more amnesty and plea bargaining.

No more paroles except by the Parole Boards; that is their job. Period. Let the Parole Boards do their job without influence.

OMG look at all the terrorists Obama has released! Talk about Treason. Yet, he has not been arrested. No one *especially* anyone representing America should be above the law.

The double-standards must be stopped, corruption stopped.

Still would love to know who let in this Trojan Horse. Who helped him into our Senate in the first place. Yes, it is relevant. We have had the wrong people coming into our Government for far too long. Go back and find out *that*, not some locker-room talk. And, look what has happened to journalism. So very sad...disgraceful even. For that matter, what has happened to our FCC?

Maybe it is because of the obscene amount of money they make, and still crave more and more, never satisfied. Why?

Did they find out a way to take it with them?

Do they think their kids will really care, depending if they get any or if the family farm that has been in the family for generations will have to be sold to pay taxes, no matter that the taxes have been paid already throughout the years.

Corruption must be stopped.

Each one of us must do what we can, no matter how insignificant it may seem. At least do something. Each one of us must vote in; or get out, the people who are making the

decisions as our representatives.

Commonsense.

Our Government could easily be

half its size and be more efficient IF

the right people are in place to do

their job correctly.

One; there are too many duplicate

programs.

Two; some programs, like

education, should be at State Level

with only one person, or Office with

three to seven at the most to

oversee the State's Education systems.

No more Tenure, get out the tired teachers, especially the ones teaching wrong!

Commonsense.

Three; our Military must be strong enough to fight and win, while being *such* that no one will want to mess with America.

Uphold standards and qualifications because it is the best thing to do. Combat ready is not about equality it is all about being the best qualified...lest we forget that, we are doomed.

Lest we forget about the loved ones waiting for their return.

Prayers for the families and friends ...

My suggestion would be to have the best training in a Military School from age 18 to 23 because the brain and most of the human body are not fully developed until then.

Besides, to risk life one should have enjoyed some life first.

Remembering to take care of those whom may pay the ultimate price of loss of life, or limbs/limitations. To be 24 to be able to go into combat. Commonsense should prevail; not whining wanna-bees.

America may be #1 at cost per student; albeit, America is 32 at actual educational levels. Sad. Very sad too that other Countries come over to America and take advantage of that which our youth take for granted.

Why should be need a Voucher System if our Public Schools are up to what they should be?

There seems to be so much lacking in our schools and too much time to do incorrect things. It can not be about money and power, it must be about the future of America; our children.

Teach them well, so they will be able to lead the way because of those role-models whom came before them to set the best examples. Yes, representatives need to be held accountable for their actions and maybe even more so for their in-actions. Corruption must be stopped.

Speaking of money and power...wouldn't it be great if Government could get things done on time *and* on budget? Those who do not, need fired. Period.

Yes, we would lose much of our Government wouldn't we?!

I bet it will work better, because to duplicate a subject does not help, even hinders it. I think that would be great, as long as you have the correct people in place.

People working for America.

People who love and respect America and whom are ready, willing and able to fight for her.

To expect less would be a failure upon those in charge; as it would be to accept less and not hold those whom are supposed to be responsible accountable.

Corruption must be stopped.

There is no excuse for failure to do a job you are paid to do. Even at minimum wage; entry level which most grow up and do better by doing such in the first place.

There does need to be either College or Trade School opportunities.

Perhaps our graduation qualifications should include a quarter or semester in the agricultural fields, literally. Proper stretching and lifting taught, of course. Like PE, a requirement. Furthermore, a semester of Music should be a requirement because of the mental and physical mind needed to learn music which helps in so many aspects of life.

Teaching Latin and Greek roots would not only help with many languages but also with the sciences. And we need more of our Americans working than to bring others over by Visa, which they usually end up abusing. there actually should be no more Visas until those here already are found *and* the proper computer to keep track of new Visas. Commonsense.

It is about People; not money and power.

Ah-ha, if you think about what you are doing the rest will come naturally…enough money and your own power of accomplishment.

After all, our children are our future. Future farmers to Representatives; and everyone in between. Each person is needed. Each person should be respected.

Our Government Employees should be at the same pay as our Military and have the same insurances. Furthermore, that there should be term limits on every position.

Being careful not to lose experience because of less pay and/or opportunity from other interests.

To be held accountable from one job to the next. Or, to help find another avenue for a job if that person needs to do so.

It is about People.

The money will come and the power to for self control hopefully also will come with the correct environment.

Communication, not riots.

Think about the different aspects to be fully committed to the passion side of life. To be where one is meant to be will be the best for all concerned in the long run.

Commonsense.

It must not be about money or power, because it does not matter which came first. What matters is to be able to take care of yourself, and then maybe a family.

Things going rough, step back, assess, make a change…move forward.

Prayers to all…

Chapter Three

Finding the Passion

Life is loving and using free-will towards a positive goal; Learning is study and research toward the true meaning of the thing to be learned; Friendship is caring and giving love in a positive way whenever possible to create the relationship necessary for self, another person, or group of people. Ladies may go to www.betasigmaphi.org to request to visit a Chapter in your area to learn about Beta Sigma Phi, a Ladies Friendship Sorority.

Men, ask your friends what positive Organization they belong to and get involved together; there are many.

Everyone can get involved in their Church, Synagogue, or Temple...sorry, don't trust Mosques because they have morals that are against the American way of life and unless they change to love America and American ways they can have no place in America.

Why come here?

If not to revel in being American.

We all have the same God and can share love as HE desires us to love one another; however, not those who hate and want to destroy us. Commonsense.

BE as a person of love because HE is in us, and we are here to fight the good fight...to fight our best fight if and when necessary.

Each of us has a right to discover our passion to contribute the best we have for ourselves and for our Country.

America.

America must come first, to then be able to help others.

We the people of the United States of America...one Nation under God...Amen

However you say that "Amen" is love to all in His sight. Amen pronounced, "Ah Mane" I believe, as it is.

Strength and Honor will prevail when you "show-up" to do your part!

Remember, nothing is free: *someone has to pay for it.*

Furthermore, you must care...for yourself and all those around you or you will pay ten-fold. Call it natural law; like gravity, or call it Karma; like wouldn't you like to see those who have wronged you get their ten-fold...however, just know that it will be...someday.

Yes, God gave us free-will, to mess up as we may; however, that is the most difficult way to learn lessons. Use commonsense.

Why not learn by other's mistakes?

What's wrong some say; thinking wrongly that there is nothing wrong in America... well, wake up America!

Money and power mean nothing if you are not a part of the solution towards making things better for all. Talking about America first. Use the analogy of putting on your air-mask first before you can assist another.

Commonsense.

With America's Debt, we must help America first or be destroyed from within. Again, the Grand Theft of American's money is unforgivable because it was mostly used to help other Countries, even those who hate America!

Talk about treasonous acts. Unforgivable.

Remember Tom Cruz in that movie, "Help me, Help you." Not by throwing fish at you, but by teaching you how-to fish.

Commonsense.

Furthermore, other countries have shown that they not only do not appreciate *it* but more so have the gall to demand more…more money, more help, more respect; when they certainly do not respect US, Americans.

Each person should discover their passion by being able to try different things to see if they enjoy *it*, or are good at *it*...both aspects must be taken into consideration when looking for the correct job. Yes, commonsense. Only then can one not just survive but actually thrive.

"The pursuit of happiness."

This "distribute the wealth" has been disproved throughout history. Pay attention.

Commonsense... Wake Up!

Edward O'Brien said, "You give a poor man money and he'll end up even deeper in debt." On that note; "Give a rich man money and he'll be the richer; so be sure to get a damn good contract." he'd kind of laugh, then get serious, "Sorry to say, handshakes don't mean much any more." then he would add, "They used to."

I think he was talking about his old-partner that took over O'Brien Industries, in San Francisco, California.

Well, maybe handshakes don't mean much anymore; so sad, *but they should.*

If a man is not as good as his word; what good is he?

Seriously, either there is trust, or not.

You know, the "old sayings" are such because they usually hold true. Think about it...

If someone steals something (or even gets something for so-called free) and gets away with it...they try it again, and again, and again... (more more more)... Then you try to teach them differently; and yes, it is so much more difficult to try to teach them how to fend-for their self.

Eventually, they get caught-up in / on the wrong side of the street/bars.

Think about it...

And then, oh-my-gosh, you end up paying ten-fold one-way-or-another.

So why not do "the right thing" in the first place?

Really, think about it...

Not to mention if a younger person sees and tries it too, because of you?

How many people might you influence around you... look around... Pay Attention...

Work smarter instead of harder (OMG, that Weiner, Huma's husband, Hillary's confidant, is still out there isn't he?) As I was saying, " Work Smart and do what is best for all."

For that matter, "Play Smarter."

Commonsense: do something right the first time and you won't have to do it again. Simple and easy.

So, what's it going to take to Communicate?

We can only do or respond to, that which we know from experience or by other's experiences. So we need to learn and become knowledgeable.

So, which do you choose, it is your choice.

Work smart, okay, let's do it together.

Not so smart, best to part company. Think about it...

That saying, "you just can't help stupid" is true; however, *wait for it*... Those willing to learn *can* achieve anything. Like others who have gone before you.

Hint: You must have the correct tools in your tool-chest /in your brain. Yes, in your brain.

You can do what you have a mind-to-do. You must take action and try.

First though, you must acquire the correct information. Check your information to be sure it is correct also. Words mean nothing without action to back them up. Sadly learned by the Nobel Peace Prize people also huh...oh yes, proven wrong.

So much has gone wrong today that it will actually take "a good Government" to start helping more. To help those single parents, lost children, rebellious and crass; to be a better person for his/herself to be able to discover their passions.

Music will help, as will PE and being involved in school.

Bring back the PTA stronger than ever, to help combat today's problems, especially in the inner cities.

We must get the Parents involved also, even with their busy schedules.

On Welfare, certainly no excuse not to be fully involved in their child's school; why not make it a requirement for aid. No, that is not a question because I am expecting some commonsense in our

Government. No, that is not too much to ask for. We the People should be demanding it. Please read again.

Make a Chart, write pros and cons or a couple of ways to approach a subject both tangible or intangible.

Most of all though, THINK…
Look over your chart and think…

Will this be best for all concerned? Then it will be good for self.

Ah ha; should you encounter something negative; just make a change. The more you are flexible to make changes when necessary the easier it will become to make changes. Just do It.

Usually the word 'just' denotes or lessons a subject OR, you can see-it-as meaning something simple to do.

The glass should always be half-full. Like in a standard 8 ounce glass of wine, in actuality 4 ounces is the healthiest. Red of course, without nitrates and sulfates.

Whichever came first; money or power?

Does it matter if you are not happy, and content with the realization that if you lost it all, that you would be fine.

Whichever, it does not really matter if whatever you are doing is not for the good of all of those concerned and you are able to discover your passion.

I remember hearing Trump asking what Dr. Carson's passion was…he said Education.

Wouldn't it be so wonderful if our teachers had a passion for teaching and our students had a passion for learning. Let us make it so.

A very good way to help both would be to teach the older children to assist the younger children. Both would learn so much more besides the grade learning, they would be helping others; therefore, they would not be bullying. Please, read again.

What is your passion?

Chapter Four

Who Am I...

If Not An American To Do My part.

Pray, Vote, Pray... **the least you can do is not near enough.**

Call me 'joe the plumber' and I will respond; for I am an American. I need no recognition, just to be recognized. I need no real money, just to be happy to be able to provide. I need no fame, just to be famous for helping those around me.

However, if I were famous perhaps I could do more good for all

concerned. Not allowing 'fame' to take control. Actors! Pay Attention.

"My Mom and I played the Lotto for years, hoping to win and be able to give the ticket over to the Veterans to have a really nice Retirement Community." No way would we have let anyone know It was our ticket.

Someday maybe our Government will learn that you can't buy friendship; however, we did not believe for a moment that money spent wrongly was anything but done

on purpose. Shameful of those
Representatives.

Unlike those sad people who rebel
and still expect us to watch them
and help the make obscene amounts
of money. Time to Boycott, even at
the harm of those around them
because they must be accepting of
their negative actions; even if by not
doing anything, that is condoning
such actions, or in-actions.

Let us not forget what really
matters...our Military we have lost on
the battlefield and those murdered
without resolve.

Reminds me of Scalia's Interview not long before his death...I still have not found the name he mentioned in his November 2015 Interview about who he would like to see follow him. Saw it on C-SPAN but could not find it again in their information.

Can you discover that information?

I can refuse to watch them or buy any of their goods that they are advertising. In fact, I can call, email, or go and see those advertisers to let them know how I feel and what I can do to do my part to help stop the

Unsportsmanlike behavior of a player or questionable conduct of an actor.

Want to leave America, go now.

Bring a Boycott sign with you if they do not want to communicate. We must all start doing whatever we can to stop the downfall of our America.

Remember when Rodman kicked the cameraman... *that* should have been the end of his career. Period.

Now, there must be examples made, to "do the right thing" to get the point across of what is unacceptable behavior because IT HAS GOTTEN OUT OF HAND!

Whatever happened to Sportsmanship?

Like Journalism too many people have taken advantage of situations and actually set a new level, *lower level,* for doing their jobs.

Number one is COMMUNICATION. How can it not be#1. The problem though lies with those to whom you are communicating. They must have proven their sincerity by actions. Sorry, not handshakes anymore.

Verbal must now be proved by actions, over time. Also, there must be matched body language and temperament....not to be fooled though, which takes time to revel sometimes. Those career Politicians whom have talked and not yet come-through should not be re-elected. Commonsense.

In the case of some; perhaps we have no better yet to do the job. Sadly, this is happening too often. My guess is that to get quality people we must clean-house and get rid of the Corruption. Certainly not to elect proven liars, thieves, or even murderers. Yes, murder by dereliction of duty is real; albeit, sadly not upheld…like too many of our laws.

Think about things and do your research prior to Voting.

Please, Thank you.

Every single 'joe the plumber' needs to Vote.

Is this not your America?

America that you love and respect.

However, it is your duty to make yourself rightly informed prior to your Vote.

Pray, Vote, Pray...

May I offer suggestions...

May I suggest you start by making sure you and our child are involved in school, and to help make our schools better whenever possible. No time; sometimes we need to make time for the more important. Remember, our children are our future, lest we forget by doing nothing.

Once you know your school, get to know your City Council and go to the meetings to find out what is really going on. There are breakfasts you may be able to meet for your Chamber of Commerce and local business people; lunches for different Political and social groups that help our community; dinners to recognize those in your community, or accepting scholarships…find those events that interest you.

Make an effort, you will be glad you did.

It is well to be informed. Make a little effort and it will mean a lot...to you and to others around you who may be involved in other things as well.

Share information.

Have facts ready and where others may find it.

My last suggestion here in this chapter would be to listen more than you speak, and to learn to speak well.

We have two ears and one mouth;-)

It really is shocking how many people, even well know people, who do not speak very well...their sentences are usually riddled with ums and ahs. Seriously, what happened to Public Speaking in our Schools, or if you missed that, take advantage of Toastmasters or some other Public Speaking group.

Practice reading out loud, besides you'll remember more too.;-)

Yes, there are those who are so blessed with public speaking skills; however, anyone can learn those skills.

Aloha Love, this may not be 'joe the plumber' however, we are all equal when it comes to being able to care and share, so Who I am to this point is irrelevant; though I am certainly not irrelevant.

Chapter Five

I Am An American Who Can Make A Difference, If I Choose To Do So. Are you?

This is a time in the History of America that needs each and every one of us to do our part. It is our duty, especially at such a crucial time.

Our government has been hijacked and being held hostage by other countries through our own Representatives in our own Government. Corruption stopped!

It is not for sure and for certain if We the People will be able to regain our America and prevent the down-fall into NWO. Lookup NewWorldOrder for yourself.

However, we must surely try. But if we fail, our 3% will fight and be shocked how many more of us will also engage.

As for now...We the People must show unity for the one man who has come out against NWO and We the People need to stand with him.

Securing our borders ASAP.

If you are not for America, you must be against her.

One of my Sorority Sisters said, his words caught on tape 11 years ago are so bad that she does not know how she can vote for Trump. Well, Sister, how can you not…at such a crucial time in America's history that will determine a future of Hello America, or Good Bye America; that is should we fail to fight along with our 3% if it comes down to that.

Pray for America…

Thinking that those 3% may not be enough since so many people against America are being planted within our unsecured borders. Our government even knows where some of the training camps are and are doing nothing about them!

Sisters: One; no I've not wasted my time to listen to guy-locker-room talk that was not meant for any lady let alone any woman; even a person like Rosie, or any foul people like her. They may act offended, but they have shown they are of *that* mentality and just rebelling.

The truth is not easy to comprehend at times. All I know is when I worked for the prison system the so-called Peace Officers talked like *that* with each other but usually said "sorry" when I was in earshot and said, "Excuse me."

No, it does not make it right, and there is no excuse for it; however, it is what it is...guy talk, not meant for women's ears. Like the saying, "Talks like a sailor." True, I've heard.

Actor Scott Baio said as much, and those who know the stakes of this election, *who love America,* are still supporting Trump. As we all need to be.

Sisters and Brothers: Two; stop with the side-show junk mentality and stick to the real problems at hand.

Ask about Policy and expect truth, finding out for yourself if it is true or not. Disregarding those lies found out about (many from wikileaks) are not allowing for proper reflection upon the stakes at hand when they have to do with our National Security and Future of America. If it is proven and in black&white, believe it. Look at that person's track-record; sorry to say, if her mouth is moving it is probably lies... but check it out for yourself.

"Sorry," really does not help and to say it over and over for the multitude of different inconsistencies and direct wrongdoings is not a Prodigal-son/daughter. And yes, it does make a difference now anyway, and always will when it comes to our People whom may be in harm's-way.

What really gets me is for a person to say she would have done something different, bull-hocky, whomever believes her; yes, you know who, is sadly so wrong and better get the right information. America is at stake!

Commonsense is that a person in a position should at least know what they are doing for that position; especially for one of the highest Offices in our Government. There is no excuse and it is Impeachable if not more so than the many reasons others are in Prison...for much less a crime than those committed by her, Hilliary.

So as an American citizen who loves this Country of ours; I must plead my case for truth and justice.

It is not just my right but my duty as an American. Communicaton.

I can get to know our Representatives from the local to the National as best as possible.

I can listen and do my research.

I must use common sense and heed those remarks not worthy of conversation being thrown at us through the New's by poor Journalism and bias reporting.

I can change the channel when it is proven that the News is bias and wasting my time. Actually, it is probably not a good idea to watch the News, except for a few; and to do my own research online. You can watch PBS and C-span usually to see the *live* coverage; however, they do not dispel the out right lies, as good Journalism would.

What happened to checking the facts *before* reporting?

What happened to our FCC?

Not inflicting their biases of course, just reporting the News…after confirming information of course. Does anyone really do that any more? I sure wonder…

When I have time, or I do make time, I sign wave and get the right fliers distributed out. I can devote an hour a day, or more, to phone calling.

At monthly Republican Women's Meeting and Luncheon we have the privilege of meeting the people running for an Office or the local Representatives giving us information about current subjects.

Whenever possible I do try to communicate with those not sure of the voting venue, who and why, and of course I do *try* to talk to Hilliary fans...only one even wanted to try to communicate though, so far.

Being a good American; I will keep trying.

Yes, it's good to hear people who are like minded; however, we must communicate with those not well enough informed. As we can show our research, and keep researching.

Please, do your own research.

I have found out that, before they know who you are for, to ask questions...about why they think their person is the best for the job...where are the facts to be found?

Know your information and that of the opponent. Of course we can not know everything, so be prepared to say that you will check it out, to get back to you; and follow-through.

That is the problem with most, the follow-through.

Who has proven to be a problem solver and follow-through with action?

Like the Ice-Skating rink in New York that the city tried to fix for years at a cost of Millions; Trump got it done ahead of time and under budget. Now wouldn't that be great for America!?

Seriously, think about the real problem-solver and how much we need him to help save our America.

Like him, his children were taught to Volunteer to help others.

Many do not know what NWO is; well do not tell them, let them look it up...because they will not believe you and they need to find out for their self.

Actually, same with most information if they are not agreeing with you. Research.

So many times you try to communicate with someone with an opposing view and they will not listen; so, listen to them first, give them your attention, and ask them questions...to confirm what they are saying is true or, maybe not...so you'll do more research and get back to them. Then, be fully armed with information, and where they can look it up for themselves.

All we can do is our best... so,

Please, do so.

Thank you.

I Am An American Who Can Make

A Difference, If I Choose To Do So.

Which try I do.

Are you a good American doing

your share?

Who Will Do What If Not I, You, or Those Who Really Care About America...

Are Those Ignoring Things are Choosing Not To Do Their Part?

We can not leave things up to the next person, we must do our own part. Look around, listen to the News, hear the wrong things being done, supposedly in the name of goodness. How absurd to believe that rioting is the right thing to do.

There is Shariah Law in America.
Heads actually being chopped off in
the name of a false god, by a false
profit for a false religion. America
must pay attention. #wakeupamerica

Less than nothing has been done
to resolve race relations which have
only gotten worse since our first
black President who was supposed
to be for hope and change; we
thought for America, however was
for other Countries. Don't take my
word for it, look it up for yourself.

Please, do your own research.

Talk about Policy and actually getting things done. A real problem solver can actually do things, instead of talking about it for years!

Wake up America, Pay Attention.

We do *not* need to talk about Military Strategies. that is for the right people and needs to be kept from the enemy. Commonsense.

When Obama tells the world we are sending 50 of our best men to...and names the place! Oh, how stupid; actually, cunning...giving the enemy information.

If you are not for America you are against her...proven so many times by this Administration.

We must give our Voice to our Representatives and when they do not listen *WE must be heard*. To do whatever it takes to get them out and a better person into that position if necessary.

Yes, not easily accomplished.

We must do our part, and not just rely on the next person to do theirs' if we are not doing ours'.

Please, do your part, then you too can have a voice because you did participate.

To show up is sometimes enough if it requires numbers; however, usually we must do more to be heard. Not riot though, of course.

We who love America and being American may try to whisper, then the other person will have to be quiet to hear.

Or, carry a sign also. Make sure it is neat and very legible.

There is no reason what so ever to yell and use profanity.

Do not stoop to that level.

Think about what *you* can do…

then, just do it…

Chapter Seven

Read over your list of what you can do from Chapter Six, and figure out different ways to accomplish those tasks.

Get together with others and do positive things for our Country, our States, your City or Community.

You have the audiences on your internet account pages. There are other groups to join and share ideas, and/or places to meet for sharing the word...

The word of Americanism.

How to save our America and how to push out NWO...

We must all do our part. Each and every one of us.

Put your ideas into action...

To be, or not to be…

A true law-abiding American will take correct action(s).

Prove it by actions, not just words. However, share as much *pertinent* information as possible.

At this time in America's History, you must act now, ASAP.

Thank you

God Bless…

Pray for America…

Mom was so involved in learning about

what was happening to America.

Sad,

Mad,

To see the downfall of America.

It seemed our Country was becoming the worst,

It's not just a neighborhood gang anymore

it's thousands of rebellious selfish whiners galore.

"Trump is right, America First!"

Mom used to also say,

"You can't help others until you help yourself first."

and

"With Trump America will be First again, someday."

Together, We the People must stand.

America First, at hand.

At 93 she had her wits' -about-her, that's For Sure

Prayers for us to meet again,

those who go before us.

To see that smile and pleasant chagrin.

RIP Mom...see you again someday...